The mushroom men

Gran liked to eat mushrooms –
little mushrooms, big mushrooms,

short, fat mushrooms and
tall, thin mushrooms.

Gran really liked mushrooms,
but now Gran will never ever eat
mushrooms.

Never ever will Gran eat mushrooms.

3

One hot day, a long time ago,
Gran went for a walk in the woods.

Gran went to the woods to pick
mushrooms for her tea.

Then, along came a big, thick, black cloud, and down came the rain.

Lots of big drops of rain fell on Gran and on her best hat and her best coat. Gran got very wet indeed!

Gran ran to the big oak tree
to get out of the rain.
But down she fell.

Crash! Splat! Down she fell
into the wet mud, and slid into the
big oak tree.

Gran hit her head hard on the big
oak tree! Gran got very upset,
very upset indeed.

"We can help! We can help!"
said the little men,
the little mushroom men.

We can make you better...

...and we can
make you clean.

Up and down they went,
up and down they ran,
all over Gran.

9

Up and down they went,
in and out they ran,
all over Gran went the little
mushroom men.

10

Gran grinned.
Gran just sat and grinned as up and down ran the little mushroom men.

Gran liked the little mushroom men.

Pen and Ben shook Gran.
"Gran, Gran! Wake up, get up,"
said Pen. "We lost you!"

"Please wake up Gran," said Ben.
"Look, the moon is out, and
it will soon be dark!"
"I hit my head," said Gran. "I hit my
head on the big oak tree. It hurt!"

"We lost you Gran. The moon is out and it will soon be dark. We must get home," said Ben.
"We must take the mushrooms home for tea?" he said.

"No!" yelled Gran.
"I will *never* eat mushrooms for tea again, *never ever, never ever!*"

13

"You must have been asleep,"
said Mum.

"You must have had a dream,"
said Dad.

"I have *not* been asleep!
I have *not* had a dream!
The little mushroom men
made me better and they
made me clean," said Gran.

To this day Gran has never had mushrooms for her tea, but she still likes to walk in the wood!